Fast Car Go
by D Perdue

How many cars can you see go down the road?

Can you count them on your fingers and your toes?

What color cars do you see? Do you see purple? Do you see green?

Are they **LARGE**?

OR

Are they *small*?

Are they *KIND*?

Or are they *MEAN!!?*

Are they fast "vroom, vroom."
Do they really like to go?
"Phewm!!! Phewm!!!"

Or are they slow "whoa!!, whoa!!"

Crash! We don't want or need any of that. Sometimes you have to go slow.

We just want to laugh...
[tickle,tickle}

Ha Ha Ha Ha Ha Ha Ha Ha HAAAA HA HA HAAA

Don't you just love watching cars go by?

My oh my how time flies.

Do you know the time?

We don't want to be late when the cars drive by.

Uh-Oh look up is that a upside down car in the sky?

How many stars can you see when you cover one eye. Now cover the other eye.

Wow that was fun
How fast can you run?

As fast as a car? As long as a mile?
As far as the sun?

Can you run backwards or even upside down? Can you flip, roll, or even run round and round?

Here they are, cars all around. In order to see them you must sit down.

Can you put these cars in order? What comes first yellow, green, or orange...is that car brown?

No!! Silly...that car is blue. It has a stripe too, it is a light shade of blue. Can you count them by twos?

2 4

6

8 10

If you had a race would you win. And if you didn't would you race again?...

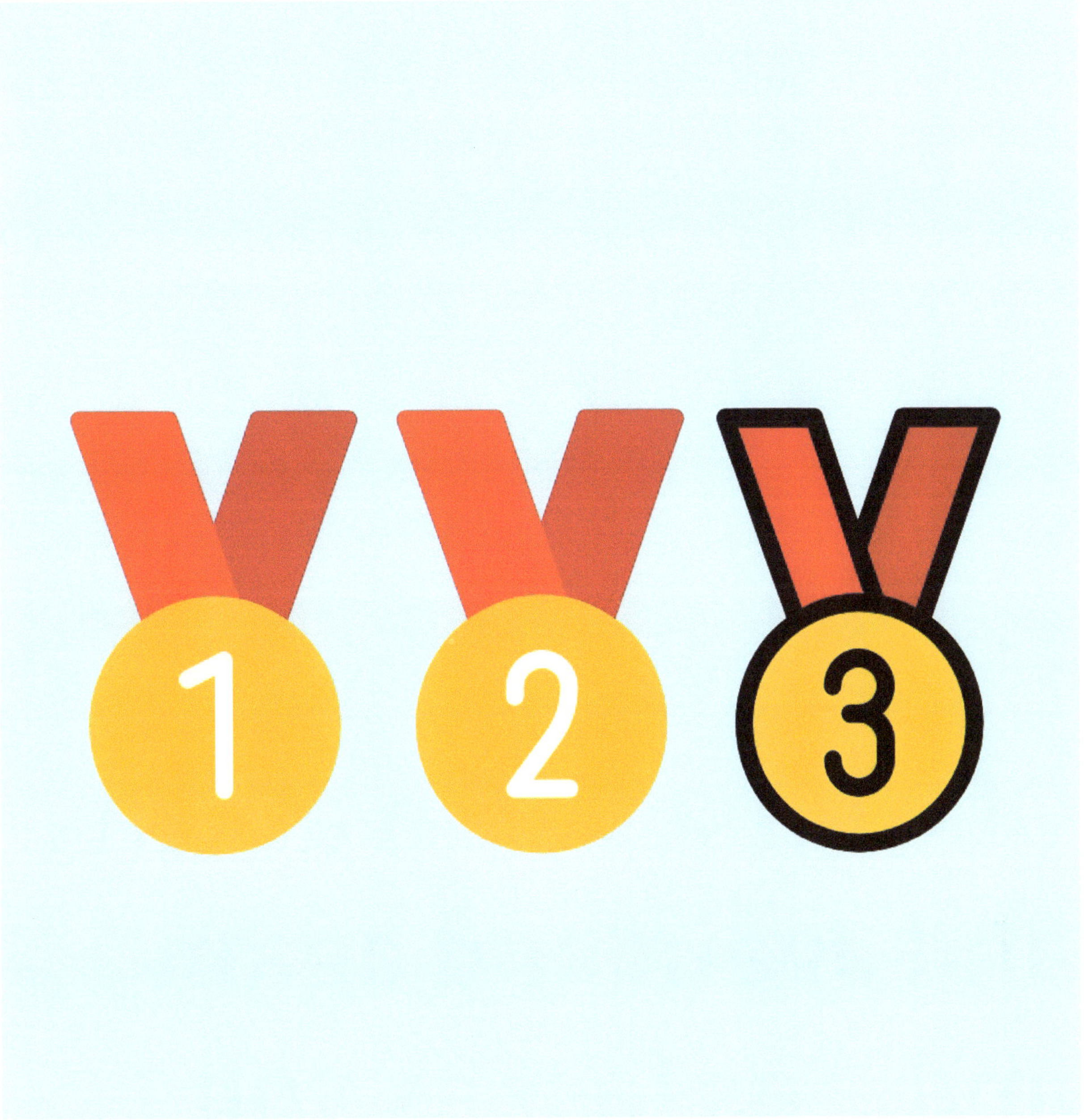
1
2
3

Of course... run again and again and again and... as fast as you can.

Now let's start all over...and do it again, and again, and again.

1 2 3
4 5 6
7 8 9 10

ACKNOWLEDGMENTS

Thank the Lord Jesus for the ability to create. I would also like to thank all those who have encouraged me over the years, it is truly a blessing to create stories. Special thanks to my wife *Rese* for always believing in me. Thank you, Bea "Bebe" Flowers for pushing me. And my special friends rooting me on all along the way. Daniel, Cindy Rich, and all the others. God bless you all. Thank you mom and dad for seeing my artistic abilities early on.

This book is dedicated to my children. Blake, Brooklyn, Breeah, Bryson, Baaron, Brylee, And my grandson Kingston.

www.ingramcontent.com/pod-product-compliance
Lightning Source LLC
LaVergne TN
LVHW071026070426
835507LV00002B/41